Social Responses to Death and Dying

Introductory Chapters

Isabelle Reedy Powell, PhD

Social Responses to Death and Dying

Introductory Chapters

Isabelle Reedy Powell, PhD

© 2019

ISBN 978107109933

Table of Contents

PREFACE

The following chapters are in response to my review of the elementary Readers that my Grandparents and Great Grandparents read during their elementary school years. Death, in those years was included in poetry and prose. During my school years, 1930 to 1941, Death was not included in the reading assignments or in the discussions. There was a consensus among professionals that it should be re-introduced into the curriculum.

My plan, for these chapters is to introduce the curriculum to gain an objective basis before entering into the more traumatic areas associated with death and dying.

Chapter 1

Basic Assumptions and Perspectives to the Analysis of Death and Dying

Introduction

Important to everyone's sense of equilibrium is a personal accommodation to one's own mortality and the development of an orientation that encompasses the meaning of life and death. Every individual organizes his death-related experiences in an attempt to place them in a comfortable perspective. The particular social group and culture of that group are significant factors in his efforts. It is during the early years of the socialization process that the groundwork for the accommodation is laid.

The development of an orientation to death and the accommodation of it was relatively simple in the historic eras in comparison to the same task today. Earlier societies were homogenous. Many of them resulted from family line, i.e. one totem. As a result, members shared the same explanation, the same orientation and the same basic beliefs. In the more primitive societies, a pattern of death-related behaviors peculiar to the group were (and are in those existing today) a clearly defined part of the ideological component of their culture.

Contemporary societies are heterogeneous and are likely to become more so in other parts of the world in the future. While there is a tendency to maintain some cohesiveness and solidarity at the homogenous level, both geographic and social mobility make interaction with groups unlike our own a likely possibility. Individuals at all age levels tend to be exposed to a variety of ideologies which relate to death and dying. Exposure to such cultural diversity demands continued reassessment and reinforcement of explanations and ways of dealing with death-related matters that were once taken for granted in a matter-fact-way.

Compounding the task of developing a comfortable perspective of dying and death is the increasing use of the explanation of death as a result of technological failure. Using technology to explain death relieves the individual of developing an orientation which allows him to place death in a functional perspective. At a time when the idiosyncratic orientation is essential to his personal accommodation to death and dying, a "cop-out" such as a technological explanation, provides an easy alternative and frees the individual from the conflict of diverse ideologies at the same time.

The American society has reached a point where the continued use of technology as an answer to life and death as well as an answer to social problems is being questioned. The use of technology frequently provokes further problems. The use of nuclear energy and the disposal of the nuclear waste is but one example. Internationally we are besought with a choice of military power or negotiation as a means of resolving conflict. Technology in some areas of science has been halted because the results are likely to lead to uncontrollable circumstances.

While technology makes up a large part of a society's cultural information, rational thought is also part of that package. With interest in technological explanation waning, rational explanations as well as predictions based in rational thought provide another alternative to the solution of problems. An individual, seeking to accommodate death and dying in his/her life experience could reinforce an idiosyncratic orientation based on theory and fact. Rational thought would demand individual involvement in accepting death as a part of life experience. The accommodation of an orientation to death may provide the sense of equilibrium comparable to that of those individuals who lived in homogenous societies.

A starting point in a rational explanation necessarily would include a definition of the concepts to be addressed. In this discussion, while death and dying will be defined in social terms, biological definitions will be used as a means of comparison. However, the focus on social aspects will be the primary concern.

Death and Dying Defined

Death is a biological and social event suffered ultimately by everyone with little preparation. It represents that moment at which one relinquishes all life support systems as well as all social roles which have been his/hers in a variety of social structures. Dying, on the other hand, is a social and biological process. We are at birth an individual who will die. In one sense we might look at life as an allotment of days. With the living of each day we then have one less of life to live, or we have spent "x" days of our life allotment. The phrase used frequently of "wishing our life away" is indicative of this dying process. At the same time, we have attained a physical maturity corresponding to the number of days lived. Thus, while the days of life decrease as each new day is lived, physical maturation increases, resulting in an inverse relationship between the two.

Life also represents the accumulation of life experiences that culminates in our social being. From the moment of birth on the healthy infant responds to others in the environment as he launches himself/herself in a unique lifetime pursuit of establishing a pattern of social relationships. It is through social interaction that he/she becomes human. During infancy this usually includes the immediate family. As he grows, he establishes other group ties, those among the members of his play group, his/her social peers and various community organizations. If he follows the usual pattern, he/she pursues a career, enters into marriage or partnership and may parent children. The nature of the relationships varies from relationship to relationship and person to person. While there are similar forms of social interaction and many social interactions will have similar content, the intensity, the complexity, the duration of social structures will vary from individual to individual. It is through our unique biological heritage and our unique social interaction history that we experience life and develop the social characteristics which identify each one of us as a unique individual. Each new day lived adds to the social interaction spent and in turn, affects our current social being.

Just as we lose a day of life as we gain a day of physical maturation, so, too, we cannot recover the day's social interaction as we gain in social maturity. Some social roles will be phased out or will lessen in intensity as new experiences command our attention. This may be the result of aging, relocation, redirection or even death. As our social structures change and we lose a social role as a result, we are in the process of dying socially. Thus, while we forfeit a day of life, we add to our physical maturity, and so too, through living we forfeit social interaction and social roles as we add to our social maturity. The price we pay for both physical and social maturity is the "x" number of days of all those allotted and the "x" number of social experiences possible in a "normal" life experience.

Death, then, is that moment when dying ends. All processes of physical and social growth are halted. In social terms, the person, previously the epicenter of social relationships no longer emits stimuli seeking response in his/her environment nor is he/she available as a recipient of external stimuli emitted in search of response. The once social individual returns to an asocial state beyond the reach of social interaction. One is as far removed, indeed, as the days prior to birth. Other than relatively short periods of self-imposed withdrawal or times when one might have suffered isolation from a person or group of persons there is no preparation for this inconceivable event that awaits every human being. We become human as a result of social interaction and the development of social relationships. Giving up of all that has made us so is letting go of life.

Such an analysis of death and dying is extremely abstract. If one has a need to visualize death in a graphic sense it might be viewed as the mirror image of life. Death immediately ends the dying process. It reflects the maturity, the day to day physical growth of the individual. While the more recent image will be the most evident, the physical development and scars of all life lived are reflected in it. Death likewise reflects the individual as a social being, as an epicenter of social roles. The social being at death is a reflection of all the life experiences from birth on, with the more recent being the most evident. Death is the event that halts both the development and dying processes both biologically and sociologically.

The family, friends, and relatives who shared roles with the deceased suffer the loss or death of the reciprocal relationship when death occurs. The response of these survivors to the death is equally difficult to describe. The giving up of those who responded to needs and added to the capacity for human expression threatens the stability of the personality reflected in that human expression. Those whose lives were enriched by a response no longer have an object seeking their response. The reciprocal pattern of fulfilling needs disintegrates profoundly, indiscriminately and with assured finality. The role, formerly assumed by the deceased in a group process is extinguished, yet the need for the role continues. Each member of the group, whether it be the family, peers, work or volunteer, is affected in some way and to some degree. When a member of a group dies, survivors suffer a personal dying experience in their loss of a social role and as a result sense a state of disequilibrium unequalled by any other group description. No experience is so frustratingly unexplainable. The social structure teeters as the loss of a human is assessed and roles are reorganized to compensate for the loss.

Death and Dying as Personal Conflict

The inverse relationships presented above represent human conflicts difficult to resolve. The price of physical maturity is the expending of life. The price of social maturity is the expending of social roles. Both expenditures can be denied. Face lifts, hair rinses and transplants may give the appearance of fewer days of life lived. Continuing patterns of childlike dependency deny social roles normally expected in relation to life lived. Nevertheless, the days catch up with us. Our existence is naturally terminal. In similar fashion both expenditures can be hastened. The young are anxious to show signs of physical maturity and wish to hasten the appearance of the number of days lived. Social interaction can result in gaining social maturity at an earlier-than-expected age. There are those whose number of social roles exceeds what an individual can comfortably cope with, some who want the world to stop so that they can physically catch up with themselves. Fundamentally, however, there is nothing we can do about this dualism. Living and dying are polar positions interacting daily throughout the life experience.

In some circumstances social roles and physical development are attained and/or ended simultaneously. Delivering an infant and the implementation of the mother role is one such example. The breast-feeding experience is another profound example. The peculiar interdependency between mother and child begins after a particular physical maturation has taken place. When the breast feeding is discontinued the social role is lost forever as is the physical development essential to that process. The sense of loss of the accompanying social role is more acute than the loss of the physical ability to accomplish it. Menopause represents a similar loss. A vasectomy, while it is artificially induced, (and today may be reconstructed), does deprive the father from entering into a father role with a natural child. These are poignant examples of what in fact occurs daily throughout our lifetimes. Life experience is paid in number of days lived and social interaction patterns completed.

These conflicts inherent in man represent two categories of human experience directly in opposition to each other referred to by Simmel as "dualisms."[1] Similar conflicts result from society's need to maintain order. Individuals choose between being compliant or rebellious, between publicity and privacy, good and evil, and so on. It was Simmel's view "that the condition for the existence of any aspect of life is the coexistence of a diametrically opposed element." Life in its absolute form is a unified entity, yet within it, a dualism between the concepts of life and death are polarized dimensions, one in direct conflict with the other. While one of the opposing factors is commonly held to be negative, it has a positive effect in that through the resolution of conflicts between the opposition, man achieves a unified personality.

Throughout one's lifetime man is confronted with dissonance between individualistic cravings and the needs and expectations of his/her environment. While there may be periods of time when one's individualism is rewarded, nature and society, as well, demand that one maintain a lifestyle in harmony with the natural and social environments, respectively. No conflict is so sharply and clearly defined as that imposed on an individual by impending death. For both the individual consciously aware of his/her fate and the survivors

---

[1] Levine, Donald N. George Simmel on Individuality and Social Norms. The University of Chicago Press, 1971.

sharing the process, the urgent nature of the event demands the placing of life and death in a tolerable perspective. All hopes and dreams of individualism are shattered. Death is obligatory and final. It is an equalizer, a common denominator. It reduces man's loftiest aspirations to the very stark realities of nature. All involved are temporarily caught in an uncontrollable current promoting imbalance and escalating pressure toward resolving the conflict.

Conflict between the self and environment will not be a new experience. What is new is the demand for submission to the event rather than to the task of maintaining a balance between individual needs and environmental demands. Man may contemporarily grope for straws to allay death, but if he/she is to achieve a sense of personal peace he must ultimately reconcile the value of life and the value of death. For a balance to be attained the pressure to face death and the need to live must be met head on as they were met similarly at the cessation of the breast-feeding process or the menopausal climatic. The acceptance of social and physical death by the person dying and the acceptance of the loss of a social role by the survivors prior to the time when death occurs is the ultimate to be attained.

Endeavors to find the means to deal with this traumatic event are recorded in the earliest written accounts of history. Evidence unearthed at archaeological sites indicates that prehistoric societies pursued institutionalized patterns to cope with the group disruption caused by death of a group member. Today, as then, part of every society's cultural information includes an explanation of why death occurs and proposed patterns of societal responses to death which are meant to provide both psychological support for the dying and the immediate survivors as well as a means to maintain the social viability of the group.

Among preliterate societies, explanations lean heavily on the prevailing ideology. In modern industrialized societies, technological is the most influential determinant in providing direction for interpretations. Both ideological and technological meanings provide avenues which may promote the denying of death or the acceptance of death.

The ideology of the Dani, a society inhabiting New Guinea, includes a legend concerning a race between a bird and a snake which explains why death occurs. According to the legend, should the snake win the race, all men, subsequently, would live as snakes, periodically shedding their skins and producing new ones to further extend their lives. In the event that the bird should win the race, all men eventually would die as birds die The bird, according to the legend, won the race and since that time, "all men must die even as birds."[2] The ideological explanation of death for the Dani promotes the acceptance of death and establishes the event as a certainty for all men. There is no way to avoid death. The ideological explanation supports the person as he/she experiences the conflict. Ideologically he/she has no choice but to submit to death, but he finds comfort in knowing that the event is natural and therefore expected by group members.

Death and Cultural Conflict

---

[2] Heider, Karl Gustav and Robert Gardner. Dead Birds (film), University of Minnesota, 1972.

In America interpretations essential to the reconciliation of the value of life and the value of death are rooted in two opposing magnetisms central to society's cultural information. This cultural conflict further compounds the personal conflicts felt by the dying, his family and friends.

Among some preliterate societies, death is seen as a punishment, the price of moral trespass of divine wrath. It may be appropriated at the will of an unknown god or, possibly, a human with special powers. The resulting death and meaning attached to the event may be used as a means of social control. Death, it is believed, can be denied and subsequently avoided by living in accordance with group laws.

In Western cultures the meaning of death, traditionally, was explained (and may be even today) in similar fashion. Man is created by God, in His image, from the dust of earth. Man is given life when God breathes life into him and man's death occurs when God chooses to withdraw the breath of life. Within such a theological structure, man found security in the knowledge that death was a personal matter between himself and God. Life was part of a divine plan. Death was a brother to life and could be confronted openly and discussed freely. It could be treated as a natural phenomenon. When man lived in accordance with the Creator's rules, he/she strove to avoid death through the avoidance of sin. He/She nevertheless recognized death as a prime requisite for life as well as an "integral dimension of personal identity."[3]

Interpretations of death in industrialized societies tend to explain death quite differently. Influenced by unmatched technological

---

[3] Fulton, Robert L. Attitudes of the American Public Toward Death, 1964.

success, the meaning and explanations of death are largely expressed in technological terms. A person dies because there is a lack of existing information to find a cure and restore good health. Individuals have no choice but to yield to death as a consequence of medical failure. Concerns, therefore, related to death, have been directed largely toward uncovering alternatives to death even as the preliterate society of the Dani sought an alternative in the possibility of shedding a skin as a snake does. While many of the more primitively oriented cultures wrote their legends and accepted death as a matter-of-fact occurrence that "all men must die", America as well as other industrialized societies perpetuate the race between the bird and the snake in their search to avoid and deny death. Modern men have generated the snake-skin approach through medical research with the ultimate goal of prolonging life indefinitely. Death is an enemy and must be denied. The fight for life must be sustained. The conflict between individualism and the natural demand of death is heightened.

Emphasis in research to accomplish the avoidance of death in modern society has moved in many directions. Modern surgery makes possible the replacement of a no-longer-efficient heart with a transplant. Life, in spite of suffering, is prolonged through various life-support systems in the hope that tomorrow will bring new solutions. Cryogenics permits sick bodies to be frozen for indefinite periods of time looking to future medical knowledge to find   a cure. The inability to allay a natural process represents a scientific challenge. Failure to provide cures and sustain life through technological means emphasizes man's severe limitations and dependence on nature. To gain control of life and the environment essential to sustenance, in modern society, is the desired objective. A loss of the ability to interact socially is ignored. Only to the extent that youth is extended through technology, longevity increased, and death avoided, can the product, the techniques, the scientific research be seen as having achieved the objective. A re-conciliation between the dualism of life and of death is not encouraged. The individual facing the loss of his/her human entity, experiences an incomprehensible discord as he/she awaits his/her fate. The survivors committed to a value of achievement and success, are faced with a conflict difficult to resolve.

The Effects of Conflict

Individuals who live in a society where interpretations of death are embedded in a struggle between ideology and technology are caught "between a rock and a hard place." While ideologies may encourage the avoidance of death, they nevertheless recognize that death is ultimately inescapable. Ideologies too, are slow to change and provide a stability that is supportive of the dying as well as to the survivors when death occurs. In a very real sense, they keep society "on track" as conflicts arise and resolutions are initiated. Technological explanations, on the other hand, are subject to rapid change requiring the individual involved to reorganize their expectations as new technical breaks are announced. The very information to cure a fatal illness may be available tomorrow! Continuing research reinforces false hopes. Resolution of the conflict may not be seen as imminent as it appeared. Many deaths of the past, to be sure, might have been avoided had present day technology been available. This is indicated by the mortality rate which is substantially lower than several decades ago. Nevertheless, death continues to be inevitable.

18

The individual in a society reflecting these opposing magnetisms faces a two-pronged battle. Though he/she may have to face death naturally, he is asked to avail himself of technology. He/she is asked to put his faith in technology, to define death in technological terms, rather than to submit to death as a natural event. Reconciliation of his/her social death, or for the survivor, reconciliation of the loss of an important figure in his/her social network is avoided. The opportunity of dying with a sense of peace and harmony is delayed or prevented. Preparation for the loss of a social role is ignored.

Attempting to explain the resulting social phenomena that have evolved as a result of the conflicting explanations and the emanating cultural patterns and practices surrounding death and dying, tease one's imagination. The contemporary social responses to death have not evolved in a vacuum. In every society the cultural information not only interprets the meaning of death but also provide a cultural configuration designed to meet the physical and emotional needs of society's members and to resolve the crisis suffered by the group affected by the loss of a member. The cultural configuration contains patterns of behavior appropriate to the event. The patterns consist of compatible social norms, standards of behavior, which are generally known and used as guidelines in determining one's behavior. The social norms reflect the values of society. When societal norms reflect compatible values, individual and societal equilibrium is supported. However, when values are in conflict, or when they are in process of rapid change, members find it difficult and even impossible to cope with a situation which requires them to focus their attention on both values at once. Professing allegiance to the value of sustaining life does not permit one to meet freely the needs of the individual who is facing death. Nor does the conflict manifested in the search to avoid death allow one to humbly and honestly face the limitations of his/her life.

The conflict between technological and ideological interpretations must be reconciled if people are to live satisfying and fulfilling life experiences. Confrontation with a problem and the successful resolution of the same are essential to mental health. The attitudes supporting the avoidance and denying of death makes for what must inevitably come naturally, if not accidentally, an unacceptable phase of life for the individual. For the survivors to avoid the confrontation of death as a loved one dies or after the death has occurred gives way to a feeling of utter helplessness and loss of control that may never be resolved. Technology historically has provided society with alternative ways of dealing with a problem. Ideology historically, on the other hand, has directed society in the selection of the alternative most supportive of society. Contemporary emphasis to technology has run any balance between the two amuck! In the concentration of efforts to find "cures" for specific physical problems, medical specialists have lost sight of the whole person. The individual's innate drive to survive further reinforces the continued research in alleviating pain and suffering as well as prolonging life. As a result, contemporary society minimizes ideological direction and a realistic acceptance of death. To avoid the risk of major societal imbalance and instability, if indeed this has not occurred already, the conflict between technological and ideological explanations must be reconciled.

American society is one of the most highly industrialized societies in the world. It is reasonable to suspect that we have absorbed as much technological information related to death phenomenon as a society can comfortably absorb. There is evidence that confidence in technology as an explanation of why death occurs as well as its role as arbiter between life and death is waning. America may have come full circle! Society may again look to ideology in search of answers. Nevertheless, whether the individuals must continue to suffer the conflict between the opposing magnetisms or if society moves in the direction of re-emphasizing ideology, either or both will result in conditions painful to society in the foreseeable future. A new rational approach encompassing both technological and ideological interpretations as well as an objective scientific analysis can serve to provide people in industrialized societies with a better understanding of the disequilibrium they sense as they attempt to reconcile these two extremely pertinent values, i.e. life and death.

Sociology

Social theory is ideally suited to study the social responses to death and dying. The discipline of Sociology is an effort to explain how society is and has been organized through the use of accepted scientific methodology. It attempts to explain social organization both from the historical perspective and the contemporary scene. It borrows the techniques use in the natural sciences to analyze social relationships and the pattern of these relationships within social organizations. Thus, with appropriate research design, data are collected and subjected to statistical analysis to ascertain the significance of the relationships existing between the given variables. However, Sociology has not always been rooted in scientific analysis. Much of early social theory resulted from introspection and is frequently referred to as "armchair sociology." While the beginnings of Sociology were largely philosophical, the idea of possible subjection of social facts to scientific analysis set Sociology apart from the philosophical leanings.

Analyzing varied and complex social phenomena has led to varied and complex social theories. At the present time no one sociological theory is available which fully explains the organization of all social relationships. Indeed, the wide variety of social theories on the surface, appear to be strange bedfellows. They are not incompatible, however. In terms of historic development of social institutions, the evolutionary theory provides an interesting framework for analysis. In explaining contemporary relationships between individuals and institutions both the structure function framework as well as conflict theory are useful. In analyzing interpersonal relationships, the symbolic interaction approach allows for detailed and precise interpretations of individual behaviors within a social relationship. The following is a brief description of social theories which provide insights to suggested questions related to understanding death and dying.

Social Evolution

Evolutionary theory is based on the premise that progress evolves in a linear fashion from a simple state to one of greater complexity. Theorists assume that the increasing complexity of social organizations is an adaptive mechanism characteristic among societies. Just as man, through physical evolution evolved to a more complex being, societies through an evolutionary process became more complex. Progress of societies is the norm. Retrogression is a rare phenomenon. Questions to which social evolution could give insight might include:

1. Do individual and/or societal responses to death and dying follow an evolutionary pattern?
2. Do specific responses coincide with specific levels of subsistence?
3. Does the funeral institution reveal indications of increased differentiation and specialization?
4. Is the care of the dying, moved from the home to the hospital to Hospice an indication of increased specialization?
5. Are there evidences of evolutionary patterns of death-related phenomena within societies? i.e. rural to urban? East to West? North to South?

4. Is there an inverse relationship between the individual's acceptance of death and social progress? i.e. from personalization to depersonalization?

5. Do the changes which have taken place within the mortuary institution reflect an evolutionary process in responding to changing values?

Structural Functional Theory

The emphasis in structure functional theory is on order. Society is perceived as a complex organization of parts, a system of subsystems. A small group such as a family is also a system with its members representing subsystems. The subsystem must function to fulfill requirements and respond to the needs of the whole. Order is maintained when a sufficient proportion of institutional and/or individual needs are met and when a sufficient portion of the institutions and the population participate in maintaining the system. Ideally the operations of the system are directed toward meeting the needs of members. When values and norms are rejected by a group or when the needs of the individuals or the institutions are not met, disequilibrium follows. Order is not achieved again until differences are reconciled. Questions that might be answered by Structure Function Theory might include:

1. How do the roles of the survivors of contemporary society differ from the roles of survivors prior to the development of the funeral industry?

2. How is the denial-of-death behavior, characteristic of members in the industrial society, functional to the individual? to the society?

3. Do responses of sympathy by friends and relatives reflect individual needs or economic achievement or, possibly both?

4. Can Voodooism be explained as a direct result of structure manipulation?

5. In adjusting to the death of a family member, how are former expectations re-directed? How are roles changed in order to experience new means of providing old expectations essential to the re-establishment of structural stability?

Conflict Theory

Conflict theory is seen by some as a special case of functional theory while others see it as a theory that must stand alone. There is the assumption that interacting individuals can be described as a social system each with his/her special positions (status) and role as is true in functional theory. Conflict, however, is viewed by the conflict theorists as a natural force of interaction rather than alluding to the fact that a social system has a tendency to remain in a steady or equilibrium state.

The theory emphasizes the social processes of change rather than order. It is assumed that all societies have both dominant and subordinate groups. Interests of one group may be in direct opposition to the interests and needs of the other group. Individuals in the dominant group are likely to have greater access to the scarce resources, i.e. power, prestige and privilege. It would follow that the members of this group would continue to benefit from the system to a greater extent than members in the subordinate group. Social order, under such circumstances, can only be maintained through manipulation, coercion and constraint. It in fact possesses the needs essential to conflict and subsequently, social change. Questions addressed in search of explanations concerning death or dying might include:

1. What are the patient's rights in decisions concerning the use of supplement-life-support systems?

2. Is the commercial aspect of the funeral a reflection of a power group?

3. Are funeral expenses related to easing the feelings of guilt a move toward Conflict Resolution

4. Can the intra-family conflicts following the loss of a family member explain the vying of power left unattended as a result of the death of a of a member who had a greater share of the system's power?

5. Is the move toward greater uniformity of cemetery monuments an attempt to restore stability in the wider social system?

Symbolic Interaction

The Symbolic Interaction Theory is rooted in two basic proponents: (1) man is responsible for his behavior. He/she has the potential to reflect on past experiences and relate them to options for response in the present. (2) Stimuli is received at the covert level, is interpreted and responded to according to the values and norms of a group. It is especially useful in explaining problems in a small group setting. Questions relating to death and dying that might be answered using the Symbolic Interaction Theory are:

1. How does dying affect the actor's interaction with the members of his/her social group?

2. To what extent are the psychological needs of the dying acknowledged through care systems?

3. Are institutionalized behaviors imposed on the dying?

4. Is "support" for the dying positive? Is "support" for the survivors positive?

5. Are the dying provided the opportunity to maintain a healthy self-image?

6. Is the relationship between the staff and the dying patient the same as the relationship between the recovering patient and the staff?

Conclusions

Sociological perspectives will enable individuals to analyze social structures more effectively. Not being born with an altruistic orientation, individuals need to be taught how to analyze a social system from the system-perspective rather than the naïve individual's peculiar, idiosyncratic, and egocentric positions.

This is particularly true at the event of death. New technologies present new alternatives. The adoption of a new alternative rarely promotes equal distribution of support to all societal elements. Conflict results and system change ensues. Ideology may furnish a guideline as the alternatives are assessed and as change is directed. Death, on the other hand, affects change directly. There is no alternative. Death is an ever-present, ever-lurking, catalyst of change. Traditionally, in order to respond to the crisis, societies have developed built-in mechanisms to assist the social groups in meeting the demands related to the death and in the group's return to stability. These responses were rooted in the prevailing ideology of the particular group. Modern societies are less likely to be so structured. It is essential today, that individuals have an understanding and an awareness of the intrinsic imbalance of a social system when death occurs so that they can function more effectively as the system vacillates. Crucial to an individual's adjustment to the loss of another is the reorganization of the structure. Only through the re-structuring of relationships can the survivors hope to receive support and nurturance essential to their wellbeing. Just as death provokes conflict and change directly, so too must man respond to the conflict directly and promote change essential to the remaining members of the social system.

The chapter which follows is a presentation of the components of cultural responses to death and dying. This is followed by a bird's eye view of cultures around the globe and their responses to conflict and disequilibrium. Non-industrialized cultures are more highly integrated than that of industrialized societies. Their integrated system of social responses to death and dying will serve as a means of comparison to those of the contemporary society.

Chapter 2

A Cross-Cultural Approach

Introduction

The birth of life, the ending of life and the accompanying physical and social maturity between the two are universal human experiences. How the society responds to these events is unique to each society. All cultures include in their ideological system an explanation of life's beginning. So, too, cultures explain life's end. Of chief concern here are the personal and societal responses to the ending of life. Wherever death occurs, it reflects a traumatic societal experience. For the dying individual, his/her future is totally out of control. No one has the power, the influence to which they can turn to allay death. They are left with little other than their beliefs and their faith in them. While they face an experience experienced by many, unlike other experiences, "none has lived to tell the tale." The survivors, on the other hand, even though the loss may be a similarly repeated experience, they too are caught in a situation beyond their control. While the belief in prayer and medical know-how may delay the inevitable, they have no power to halt the on-coming loss and must ultimately submit to it. When death occurs, they suffer a state of disequilibrium unequalled by any other group event in normal circumstances. It is the purpose of this chapter to give insight into the societal responses (cultural components) related to death and dying. These responses are a part of each society's culture throughout time and space.

Culture defined

It was not until about 1900 that the term "culture" was used to refer to a way of life for a group of people. For a period of time, while the components of culture were studied, there was a tendency to rank cultures as having more or less culture. Today, both anthropologists and sociologists aspire to the perception of "cultural relativity." They endeavor to study the components of culture, one component in relationship to another and all in relationship to the physical and social environment of the group rather than to compare a specific culture to their own. Pelto and Pelto define culture as "the systematic patterns of explicit and implicit concepts for behavior and for behavior settings learned and used by individuals and groups in adapting to their environment.[4]

This is not to say that all members share equally in the whole configuration of a culture. There will always be some individuals who have idiosyncrasies. In a large society there will always be small groups, subcultures, who practice certain behaviors peculiar to the

---

[4] Gretel H. Pelto and Perri J. Pelto, The Cultural Dimension of the Human Adventure, N. Y. MacMillan, 1979, p.42.

larger group. Culture refers to that configuration of learned beliefs, values and behaviors generally shared by members of a society.

The components of a culture make up a system, each component being a subsystem interrelated with the other subsystems. Each is subject to change as the needs of the group change. The subsystems of cultural system identified by Williams are: (1) the social relations subsystems: (2) the linguistic system; (3) the technological subsystem; and (4) the ideological subsystem.[5] Each one of these subsystems includes a large number of categories or patterns. The subsystems of social relations would include all those patterns of relationships which normally exist between group members. They provide the group social structure, a stable system of response generally taken for granted by the participants. Family patterns, child rearing patterns, as well as death and dying patterns are but a few of the many that could be mentioned.

The patterns of social relations that take place when a group member dies would include: (1) the behavior patterns related to the acceptance and care of the dying; (2) the behavior patterns related to the disposition of the body; (3) the behavior patterns related to the re-establishing of social stability; and (4) the behavior patterns related to the mourning process. Each would include patterned ways of behavior between the immediate survivors and as well as between the immediate survivors and the wider community. Each of the above group patterns can be identified as a social system in its own right. The total set of institutionalized behaviors results in a complex

---

[5] Thomas Rhys Williams, Introduction to Socialization, St. Louis: C.V.Mosby, 1972, p.11.

network and will vary from culture to culture and from subculture to subculture in the larger society.

Behavior patterns related to the acceptance and care for the dying in the various cultures cover the entire range of possibilities from close and personal contact to the time of death, to group support for isolating the dying. There are instances where the dying appear to perceive their oncoming death and make an effort themselves to notify friends and family of the doleful event. The group surrounds the ailing member. Dying is talked about. Considerations for wishes following one's death are voiced. At the other extreme a group member may be removed to a dying hut or a sterile hospital room where the dying member dies in isolation. Whatever the custom, the institutionalized pattern is generally compatible with the total cultural system.

Patterns of disposition of the body are just as varied. Bodies sometimes are weighted and tossed into the river. Others are interred or cremated. Some cultures expose the corpse to the elements, others to hyenas or other animals of the forest. Some return to the corpse to recover the bones to be left in a special place so they may be shown continued honor and respect. Some cultures eat the flesh of the dead, some partake of the ashes following cremation. Deceased children customarily are treated differently and not accorded the respect and dignity ordinarily shown the adult. Again, regardless of the cultural pattern, the disposition is seen as appropriate by the group and is in accordance with the cultural system.

A study of the survivors and their response to the death of a family member or a group member as they set out about re-establishing the social stability of the group takes many forms also. The chief purpose of the funeral is to acknowledge that a group member has died and to initiate momentum toward the development of a new social structure. Feasting is an important means of accomplishing this. If the kin group had an established hierarchy, the new "head" is so designated. Gifts to the survivors or in memory of the dead strengthen ties but also provide undercurrent obligations which reinforce a social structure. Many

cultures have seen a surviving widow as one with few or no opportunities for rebuilding a social structure. Various cultures have institutionalized patterns to resolve this crisis. The Indian "suttee" is probably more widely known. Following the death of a husband, his body is cremated ritually. In the past the living widow (or widows) was required to throw herself on the funeral pyre to join her husband's burning corpse. Should she not have had the courage she would have been assisted to do so by survivors. Among the Tiwi of Australia the widow is immediately married at her husband's graveside to another member of the tribe.[6]

Mourning behavior to a member's death provides a fourth dimension in the study of patterns related to death in the subsystem of social relations. Frequently, societies divide themselves as mourners and non-mourners, with assigned roles for each group. Designated individuals prepare the body, dig the grave, carve the grave marker. Individuals may be employed to openly mourn the loss of a member. Appropriate attire for family members may be specified. Indicators of a loss of a family member may be placed

---

3 C .W .Hart and Arnold Pilling, The Tiwi of North Australia, N.Y.:Holt, Rinehart and Winston, Inc. 1960, p.18

outside of the family abode. Foreheads and legs may be slashed allowing blood to run freely and dry as it forms rivulets on the face and body. Fingers of a surviving female child may be chopped off. The previous home of the dead or parts of it may be burned. The social relations system of the cultural configuration of death-related phenomena is a good example of the cultural diversity which has evolved to cope with necessary individual and social adjustments.

The subsystem of language includes three means used by a culture to convey information from person to person: (1) gestures or body language, (2) spoken language, and (3) written language. Communication patterns seen as acceptable in relaying information about the loss of a loved one varies in form as do the patterns of social relations above. The slashing of the forehead is a gesture denoting anguish. The "rending of clothes" by Orthodox Jews is a similar gesture. Wearing of black clothes, veils and black armbands communicate to the group that a survivor is suffering grief. Loud wailing, certain calls, tolling of bells and drumbeats communicate the event of death. Written language permits the event as well as plans concerning the event to be published for the present and future generations. Feelings are expressed through poetry, folklore, personal notes and music. Vocabulary develops as new information is received and shared. Among the Bushman of the Kalahari Desert there is a word in the vocabulary which means "to have been buried alive yet living." In this area where technology to ensure one that death has occurred is rare, being buried alive and surviving the ordeal is not unusual. This necessitates a word to communicate the event. Expression through language whether it is through gesture, speech or written is an important component of each society's culture and evolves in accordance with other subsystems of a specific culture.

Technology is the subsystem of culture that enables man to survive within the limitations of the natural environment. This component is ordinarily identified with the sustaining of life, i.e. the means of acquiring food, providing shelter and clothing, the means of production and distribution, transportation and other such necessities. Technology, however, is necessarily related to death also. This is particularly true in predicting the cause of death and the care of the dying prior to death. It is also true in determining the alternatives relative to the disposition of the body. Disposition of the body is extremely simple where technology is limited. Placing the corpse in tree branches high above the ground or placing the body on the highest available hill where the fowl of the air clean the bones of flesh is not uncommon. Neither is it uncommon to place the body in a shallow grave. While death is a leveler of man the available technology within a society and the wealth of the individual who died are reflected in the alternative plans concerning the preparations made for the disposition of the body. Graves may be lavishly designed as is true of the great pyramids of Egypt and the cathedrals of Medieval Europe. Whether or not the body is embalmed may be related to technology and wealth of the dead. The time sequence between the death, the interment and the rituals may be dependent on the same variables. In generalizing cultural characteristics related to technology, it is necessary to distinguish between the cultural differences of the existing classes when they are highly differentiated in lifestyle practices.

The subsystem of ideology includes the information of a culture that is used to interpret experience and give meaning to life. Man's behavior is not determined by instinct, but rather by past experiences and his evaluation pertinent to a given situation. Ideology provides him with guidelines for selecting appropriate avenues following the evaluation. The subsystem includes cultural beliefs, values and norms which have evolved within a given society. Beliefs provide answers for unexplainable experiences. This would include an explanation of why death occurs as well as how life begins and what happens to life after death. It would also establish the time at which life begins, - before birth, at birth or at an interval of time following birth. Values are important in the selection of alternatives regarding these vital points during the life process as well as many routine decisions during the lifetime experience. They make it possible to prioritize available choices. Life itself and who has the right to live are ever prevailing problems in all societies. Among various populations where there is constant uncertainty of ample food, infanticide is valued, as difficult as the choice may be. Other people in similar circumstances value the young and support suicide of the elderly family member. In America there is continued controversy concerning life or death for the murderer with some questioning whether death is in fact less punitive than life imprisonment.

Further indication of values is evidenced in the material objects used to convey the values of esteem and respect. The objects placed in the grave of the dead were associated with the deceased's position within the group. In contemporary society, the kind of ceremony planned in conjunction with the disposition of the body or in memory of the dead and the material objects used during the ritual, serves the same function. Flowers, memorial contributions and other means of conveying sympathy to the more immediate survivors of the dead are yet other indicators or material values.

The expression of these values is revealed in the norms. The adorning of the corpse with woven bands is a norm among the Dani of New Guinea. Embalming the dead Pharaohs of Egypt was a norm of that culture. The observable behaviors usually displayed in similar circumstances are norms. The essence of the norm is rooted in values cherished by the group which in turn are rooted in the belief system.

The four subsystems of social relations, language, technology, and ideology are closely intertwined. It may be assumed that all the patterns rooted in these subsystems evolved from human and group needs. The ways by which these needs are met within a culture are determined by the special values that give meaning to the event. It appears that in almost all societies a supportive community at the time of death is seen as important. Memories of the dead are cherished. In most cultures the opportunity to express grief openly is valued. Other values might include the reassurance of life after death, the overt expressions of appreciation for the life that was; a period of adjustment and understanding as one attempts to redefine one's role. And of course, the proper disposition of the body has been valued since the appearance of the Neanderthal Man thousands of years ago.

In time patterned ways of meeting needs are looked upon as appropriate responses. Roles are defined. The widow or widower is assisted in playing the role according to the norms of the group. The eldest son, other children, the group members who are either leaders or have some expertise in the preparation of the body and the disposition of it all respond in somewhat automated fashion according to their status and ascribed roles. Some patterns will be less beneficial than others to the survivors. Some will give greater satisfaction than others to the participants. New technology may enhance "old" ways.

Patterns may bend to make room for new ways to care for the age-old problem of dying and death. But institutionalized patterns are slow to change and even when they may be detrimental to the dying process or to the support needed for the survivors, institutionalized patterns may stubbornly persist. A review of the Hindu funeral reveals the multiplicity of traits within the various subsystems.

The Hindu Funeral[7]

Hinduism is the religion of the vast majority of Indians. When a Hindu is seen to be approaching death, the Joint Family is called together to be with him when death occurs. The presence of grandchildren, and especially great grandchildren are seen as being especially auspicious. It is not seen as being appropriate for a person to die in his bed. He instead is placed on a mat or on straw on the floor. *Kush* is the purest grass and is preferred in this ritual because it is said to be "very holy." Other materials from the thatched roof or straw mats on the floor may be used. The important characteristic of the grass is that is must be dry.

Hindu families keep a covered jar of holy water from the river Ganges in the household for use in religious rituals. At the time of death some of the holy water is put into the mouth of the dying person. While water from the source of the Ganges in the Himalayas is preferred, the water of the Ganges collected at any point is believed to be pure. It is said that water from the Ganges can be kept in a

---

4 Isabelle Powell, The Hindu Funeral. Interviews with Professor R .P .Sharma, Regional Officer, U. S. Educational Foundation in India; Professor D .P .Apte , Registrar Gokhale Institute of Politics and Economics, Pune; and Mr. S.A. Patanker, Tilak College of Education, Pune, July 1980.

covered container indefinitely without becoming impure. The Ganges is a vital part of Hindu history. It is seen as the source of life. Civilizations have flourished in the river valleys. It flows throughout the plains and irrigates the fields. Hindus are expected to bathe in it at least once in their lifetime. Many who live along its banks perform this pattern of spiritual renewal weekly. When plans for the disposal of one's body are discussed, many ask that their ashes be cast upon the surface of the Ganges. The river not only is valued as the source of life and the symbol of spiritual renewal but also, in the death of loved ones, has an emotional attachment for them. Following the application of holy water, a "speck" of gold is chipped from any gold item available and placed on the tongue of the dying person. This is a means of assuring the dead's entrance to the golden steps to heaven.

Plans for the disposition of the body are entered into immediately. The body may be kept in ice if available but ordinarily it is cremated on the day when death occurred. In rural areas the entire village enters into the expression of sorrow. In larger towns and cities, the communication of the death to friends and relatives and the time needed to gather at the family home may take as much as three to five hours. No food is to be eaten during the time between the death and the disposal of the body. The period is one of extreme sorrow. This is evidenced by wailing and the rolling about on the floor. The immediate family is to do no work. So important is this to the neighbors so that even those who have not been on speaking terms join in the other neighbors in offering their services. Small children are taken to the homes of friends where they are taken care of for the interim period.

A stretcher, the *thathari*, is made of two long bamboo poles with smaller ones placed crosswise and secured with rope. Dry grass is spread over the stretcher. A loin cloth is put on a man's body and after being placed on the grass is wrapped and tied with a white sheet. If the deceased is a woman, her breast is covered also, and she is wrapped similarly but in a red sheet.

The oldest son lifts the body and is then assisted with four pallbearers, each placing one end of the poles on a shoulder. The body is moved with the feet toward the South, the head to the North. There is a legend that a king of Sri Lanka stole the wife of Rama, one of the chief Hindu gods. Since that day, South has been seen as the direction of the devil. To the North, on the other hand, is the Polar region, the Himalayas and the source of the Ganges, all representing purity. The villagers and friends collect dried cow dung and carry it to the site of the cremation. This is to be used for fuel. The village barber takes fire in an earthen pot for lighting the pyre. Thus, the procession proceeds with the family priest leading the way. There may be men following him with musical instruments. Being carried by sons or other close relatives and friends is considered the most appropriate means of transporting the corpse. However, others may assist as they process. In more recent times the corpse has been placed on a truck flat to be drawn by oxen or auto. In certain areas a funeral hearse is available which can be hired for about twenty rupees (About thirteen United States dollars in the year 1980). While these latter means of conveyance are a convenience, they are not readily acceptable to the Hindu people. As parents carried one as a child, so should the children be willing to carry their elders in death.

Relatives and friends follow the *thathari,* men immediately behind, the women trailing the procession. Many carry flowers and toss them on the corpse and stretcher. Recitations from the "Veda" or "Geeta" about the philosophy of life and death or the transmigration of the soul are uttered by anyone who so desires. Close relatives will chant in the original Sanskrit:

> *"Ram nam sadya*
>
> *Sadya hei to gadi she."*

Which translated is:

> "The only truth is the name of the Lord
>
> If you stand by the truth you achieve salvation."

Much chanting continues until the cremation site is reached. After leaving the home a certain place on the way to the cremation site is identified as the *pind.* Kneaded cakes of barley flour are placed on the chest of the corpse in a brief ceremony designating the *pind* as the place where the dead forgets his earthly home and thinks of his home of the future. From this point on, he will look forward and never again, backward.

The cremation sites are stationary. If a river is within a reasonable distance the cremation site will be on its banks. There are some areas where this is not possible and other sites are so designated. The funeral pyre varies depending on the financial resources of the family. The most valued fuel is sandalwood with substantial amounts of *ghee* or purified butter, and incense. The odor from the sandalwood, *ghee* and incense do not affect the environment or people adversely but are conducive to both mental and physical health. The addition of these three ingredients is part of the sacred cremation ceremony. For those not able to afford sandalwood, other woods and dried-cow-dung - bricks are appropriately used. When the funeral pyre has been prepared, the *thathari* and sheets are discarded (These are believed to be "unclean.") and the body is placed upon it with more wood or other fuels covering the loin-wrapped corpse. The eldest son has the first claim to light the pyre. However, should he not be available, another son, a grandson, a brother or a friend, in that order may have the honor. Whoever is given this honor, is dressed in simple white clothes, and must be shaved by the village barber of all hair, both of head and beard before the pyre can be lit. He is to observe austerity during the ceremony and throughout a thirteen-day mourning period, think "no evil thought" and is required to sleep on the floor for thirteen nights. The person selected for this function has the most important duties of the death-related ceremonies both those immediately at hand and the death related ceremonies of the future.

The body is reduced to ashes in three to five hours. Relatives and friends may wait out the process. This is usual in rural areas, however in urban areas they return to their homes for a period of mourning. The person who lit the pyre will return to the cremation site on the second day to collect the ashes and bones. On the third day these may be immersed in the river by the cremation site or other designated areas. Allahabad, where the Ganges and the Yamunna rivers converge, is seen as the holiest place by the Hindus. For the Buddha the holiest place is the Goya, near Putna, for the Ujjain, central India; for the Sikkh, Bombay. Persons may request where their ashes are to be scattered. Prime Minister Nehru asked that half of his ashes be scattered over the plains of India and half in the Ganges. The ashes of the late Sanjay Gandhi were scattered in four areas to which he had strong attachments and political followings. The bones and ashes may be kept by the family indefinitely until such time as a family member can travel to the site most revered by the deceased.

Electric furnaces are available for the cremation ritual but are unacceptable to the Hindu people who see this procedure as a disservice to the departed. The expense is but twenty to forty rupees as opposed to two hundred rupees for the burning at the usual cremation sites. There is a tendency for the better educated in Pune to use the electric furnace. For them they see "no big difference." Others, however, feel so strongly that the open cremation only is appropriate so that money is borrowed, if needed, to make this ritual possible. While the very poor, particularly in rural areas, will bury their dead, this heretofore has been seen as shameful by the Hindus. These lower-class families today may opt to use the electric cremation since it costs considerably less. Babies, and even children of eleven or twelve years frequently are buried or tossed into the river with little ceremony. Those who die with infectious diseases such as smallpox are weighted with rocks and carried into the river for disposal. In 1980 a bus accident occurred in South India which was fatal to its many occupants. The bodies were weighted and disposed of in a river to facilitate the disposition of so large a number. Several days later the bodies surfaced causing a very serious problem.

Many superstitions plague the survivors as they return home. They may be polluted and so wash their hands and feet before entering their home. Bitter leaves from the Neem tree are chewed for their disinfectant and medicinal characteristics.

Mourning continues for thirteen days if the deceased is male, eleven or twelve in the case of a woman. The first three days are a period of deep mourning. No fried foods but only "simple foods", cooked or baked are eaten. On the third day, if the day is one during which ceremonies can occur, close relatives and the larger family gather to eat at the house of the person who died and take part in a small ceremony. The person who lit the funeral pyre will return to the *pind* and leave food there. When he returns, all will eat. Some offering is made to the soul, which according to the Hindu beliefs never perishes. The priest attends the ceremony to purify the whole family. This day marks the time when the restrictions related to deep mourning are lifted and some of the regular functions and life's activities may again take place. During the next ten days the family does not mingle with friends. (In the past they very well might have been contaminated and their isolation may have served as a means of protection for the remaining societal members.) For those who can afford it, recitations will be offered from the "Upanishad" Eighteen Puranas", Garud Puranan" and other religious books and philosophies.

On the thirteenth day the ceremony *derahvin* takes place. This is the Feast of the Brahmins, thirteen priests representing the thirteen days of mourning. If the person who died was old or very ill, grief will be less, and a huge feast will take place. Should the deceased be young or one who has given much service to his people, the grief will be deeper and there may be no feast at all save the feeding of the thirteen Brahmins. The person who lit the funeral pyre will again return to the *pind* and again, after his return, the feast, large or small, will take place.

Hindus all over the country, use the Hindu Lunar Calendar. The calendar does not have the usual 365 ¼ days and results in an additional month, *ashwin* every fourth year. It is divided into two fortnights, one half during the period of the ascending moon and the second period, the descending moon. The fortnight when the moon is declining is a dark period called *shraddha paksha*. During this period ceremonies in the name of all who have died in the family must be performed. The souls of the departed return to the place from where they departed and expect the same of the living. *Tarban*, a water offering, and *Kush*, grass valued for its purifying power are offered to the departed souls followed by a food offering. The family is reminded that the soul never perishes, that the family always has obligations to the departed souls and that the souls must be gratified. If the family is financially able, they will feed the priests on the day commemorating the death of the family member, perform certain religious functions and give alms to the poor. On the fifteenth day a collective ceremony takes place where water offerings are bestowed to all ancestors. It is at this ceremony where the sacred Brahman thread is changed in a purification ceremony.

In some areas of the country ceremonies such as the death ritual and even condolence visits are seen as inappropriate on certain days. By the same token, if a person dies on a festival day, that celebration will not take place until a child is born on the designated festival day. The day of the feasts of lights is one such example.

Conclusion

This account of the Hindu customs surrounding death can be categorized into groupings of cultural traits. Classificatory schemes enable the observer to quickly denote differences between groups. Variations from rural areas to urban areas, from one religious group to another, from one subculture to another, from one geographical area to another, from one period to another, offer meaningful insights into potential for change from the traditional to contemporary expressions. There are several indications of such change in the account above: the use of oxen-drawn carts to auto-drawn carts, to the use of a hearse to transport the corpse; option to use the electric furnace by the educated as well as those who choose this means of cremation because of limited financial assets. There have been occasions when because of business responsibilities, the person designated to light the pyre has asked that he be spared the shaving of his head. The request was granted. In certain areas the feasting on the thirteenth day is questioned. Generally rural areas do not have the liberty to abandon their traditional customs. In the cities, however, there is the beginning of a new ideology. That which is most practical and efficient is becoming more acceptable. These values related to technology may become more significant in the future as India continues to progress as an industrialized nation.

Chapter 3

Conflict Responses to Dying and Death in Earlier Societies

Introduction

Of interest to the discussions of contemporary social responses to death and dying, is a comparison of[8] practices reported by anthropologists in earlier societies. Three earlier societies identified on the basis of survival technology are the Hunting and Gathering Societies, Horticultural Societies, and Agricultural Societies. There is evidence in these societies that social responses to dying and death took place in structured patterns to allay the process of dying and to ease the conflict resulting at the loss of a member. There is evidence also that the level of survival technology influenced the social responses to death and dying.

---

[8] See bibliography*****

Death and Dying Patterns among Hunting and Gathering Societies

Speculation might lead one to think that circumstances associated with the technological means of acquiring food could be related to death and dying and the customary responses when a death occurs. In Hunting and Gathering Societies the food- supply is generally limited. Survival is contingent on the day-to-day kill and such roots as may be in season. Tools are limited as well. While the bow and arrow, the spears, and in some societies, crude knives are commonly used, the tool for digging is the digging stick, little more than a pointed segment of a small tree trunk. Their nomadic lifestyle would prevent them from having a central location for burial. Nevertheless, when death occurs, they may feel it necessary to respond quickly, to get on with the business of living and allow flexibility in behavioral patterns as may be dictated by materials attained in the area.

In Hunting and Gathering Societies, perpetuation of the group is given precedence over the individual. An individual's life, then, is important only if it does not pose a threat to this goal. When a female infant threatens the adequate food supply and care essential to the members of the group, infanticide is seen as acceptable. In some groups, suicide of the elderly is valued. Abandonment of the sick and aged has been practiced by many societies. Because of the moves between campsites necessary to locate a new stock of food, traveling would become more and more difficult for the old and infirm. Falling behind was usually initiated by the aged themselves but was also enforced at times when the survival of the stronger and healthier were threatened. Among some Alaskan Eskimos, suicide is ritually encouraged and initiated.[9] It is reported that the chief cause of death among the Kwakiutl Indians in British Columbia is drowning but this is viewed as being suicidal rather than accidental.[10] Members of these societies generally enjoy life, hard as their existence might be, but readily accept death as a normal part of life and as a functional and necessary event essential to the life-chances of the group.

Several common threads of response can be identified when death occurs in Hunting and Gathering Societies. Disposition of the body takes place very quickly. Some groups contrive death to take place beyond their camp, hereby avoiding any involvement in the disposition of the corpse. The Salish Indian Fishermen of the Northwest send their dying in the company of an old man of the forest. There the dying one confesses his misdeeds and then is assisted in locating himself in a fork of a tree, where he may die at peace without the possible abuse of attack by hungry animals.[11] Nance reports similar behavior among the Tasaday of the Philippines. During his stay, a young boy was left to die, and Nance, taking pity on him, administered some of his own antibiotics. The boy regained his health and rejoined the group with little fanfare. When a Tasaday, in company with another, dies away from camp, his body is covered with leaves and left on the spot where death occurred. [12] The Tiwi of Australia bury their dead wherever the death took place also. Their dead are wrapped in tree bark and interred within a 24-hour period.[13]

---

[9] Edward Weyer, Jr., "The Eskimos: Their Environment and Folkways", New Haven: Yale university, 1932, p.249.

[10] Ronald Rohner and Evelyn Rohner, "The Kwakiutl: Indians of British Columbia", N.Y.: Holt, Rinehart and Winston, 1970, p.52.

[11] Dale V. Hardt. "Death: The Final Frontier", N.J.: Prentice-Hall, 1979, p. 95

[12] John Nance. "The Gentle Tasaday", N.Y. Harcourt Brace Jovanovich, 1975, p.396.

Flexibility in the methods of disposition can be documented by various groups. Few Eskimos are buried. The ground may be frozen to a depth of one to two feet making it impenetrable. Cremation is acceptable but rarely is there an oversupply of fuel allowing this luxury by their standards. The corpse is frequently cast into the sea or placed on a floating piece of ice. Some, when circumstances permit, are placed in wooden boxes which are then placed on wooden posts. Outright exposure is yet another common means of disposition. Limbs of the corpse, in this case, are lashed to the body which is then removed from camp. It may be surrounded by a circle of rocks or covered with rocks. It is anticipated that animals will pick the flesh off the bones. Should interment be a possibility the corpse may be buried in either a flexed or extended position.[14] The Aleuts bury their dead in a flexed position, lying on one side, the head stained with red ochre. They may include grave linings of whale shoulder blades and flat stones and place chinks of whale bone over the corpse. Labrets (lip jewelry) frequently adorn the body.[15] The Cheyenne dress the corpse in the deceased's finest clothes and wrap it in furs or blankets. The "bundle" may be placed in the crotch of a tree, placed on a scaffold or may be left on the ground and covered with rocks.[16] Other Plains Hunters allow similar flexibility. Wisner notes that "each tribe tolerated several forms of burial."[17] The Blackfoot Hunters, for

---

[13]   C.W.Hart and Arnold R. Pilling, "The Tiwi of North Australia", N.Y.: Holt, Rinehart, and Winston, Inc, 1960, p. 90.
[14]   Dale V.Hardt, op.cit. p. 95.
[15]   William S. Laughlin, "Aleuts: Survivors of the Bering Land Bridge", N.Y.: Holt, Rinehart, and Winston, 1980, p.89.
[16]   E. Adamson Hoebel, "The Cheyenne: Indians of the Great Plains", N.Y.: Holt, Rinehart and Winston, 1960, p. 86.
[17]   Clark Wissler, "Indians of the United States", N.Y.: Doubleday & Co. Inc., 1940, p. 304.

example, after dressing the corpse and painting the face, may have placed it in a fork of a tree, in a ravine, or on the summit of a hill and covered with rocks and dirt. At times a warrior's horse carried the corpse to a cave where it was killed and interred with the corpse.[18] The Comanche, also Plains Hunters, used caves as well. Hoebel reports the story of a young and poor youth who in an attempt to rob the deceased of his silver earrings awakened the corpse interred in a cave. After the informed survivors retrieved the interred warrior, the youth was not punished for grave robbery but rather was given the fine clothes of the revived man and four horses.[19]Newcomb states that among the Subartie Hunters and Fisherman "several methods of burial were practiced, including placing the dead on scaffolds built on poles or in trees...burial in log tombs" all probably associated with the difficulty of digging graves in frozen soil.[20]

When the internment is the choice for disposition the gravesite is usually protected in some fashion. The Semang, fisherman of Malaya, dig a narrow trench, place the body in it in an extended position and arrange some bamboo sticks over the face to prevent dirt from getting in the eyes. Plants are planted on the grave and a roof placed over it to protect it from the rain. In addition, a fence is built to keep animals away.[21]The Mardudjara of Austrailia tie the limbs to the body but leave the left arm free to chase away wild Dingoes. They also cover the grave with logs, branches and stones.[22] The Salish Indians build a

---

[18]   George Bird Grinell, "Blackfoot Lodge Tales",Lincoln ,Neb.:University of Nebraska Press, 1962, p.194.
[19]   E. Adamson Hoebel, op. cit. p, 86
[20]   William W. Newton, Jr.. "North American Indians: An anthropological Perspective", Cal.: Goodyear Publishing Co. Inc., 1974, p.118,
[21]   Robert Knox Denton, "The Semang: A Nonviolent People of Malaya", N.Y.: Holt, Rinehart and Winston, Inc., 1979, p.90.

---

fence around their graves.[23] In Morgan's "Indian Journals" he records that "The Chippews usually bury their dead in a sitting position and build a roof over the grave. Through the door at one end, food was placed by the grave. Through the door one could talk to the spirit of the dead."[24] He reports that the Kaw, the Sawk, the Foxes, the Cheyenne, the Shawnee, all in Kansas, have similar burial customs. Gravesites frequently are protected against animal molestation and are rarely marked for permanent identification.

While the urgency for quick disposition may be related to the need to get back to the business of living, the hasty response may also reflect the awesome fear of the evil spirits or ghosts, possibly remaining in the presence of the corpse. The "funerals" of the Washo, Indian Gatheres in California, in fact were not ceremonies designed to honor the dead or to comfort the living, but rather to ensure the survivors that the dead person's spirit would not return. The brief Washo prayers were really exhortations to the dead person to accept his death and leave the living alone. The burial was initiated quietly and quickly.[25] The Sauk, after the body is set up in the grave is addressed and reminded "You must not come back to trouble us who are left behind, but leave us in peace."[26] The Cheyenne believe that the ghost will not start to journey to the Milky Way until the body has been removed to its final resting place.[27] What little ceremony takes

---

[22] Robert Tonkinson. "The Maradudjara: Living the Dream In Australia's Desert", N.Y.;Holt, Rinehart and Winston, 1978, p.83.
[23] Dale V. Hardt, op. cit. p. 95.
[24] Lewis Henry Morgan. "The Indian Journals", 1859-62, Ann Arbor: The University of Michigan Press, 1959, p.82-83.
[25] James F. Downs, "The Two Worlds of the Washo", N.Y.: Holt, Rinehart and Winston, Inc., 1966, p.59.
[26] Lewis Henry Morgan. Op.cit. p.83.

place following the death of a group member of the Mardudjara is for the purpose of ensuring the permanent separation of the spirit from the living.[28] The Semang place their fires at the head and the foot of the grave to ward off evil spirits and the survivors are expected to participate in rituals to protect them against evil spirits.[29] The Aztecs enter into ritual dances to scare off evil spirits.[30] Children or the ill are seen as the most likely to be influenced by a ghost who may want company and frequently are kept indoors or protected symbolically. It may be the urgency of disposition is related to additional deaths among group members and the group's recollection of the additional losses following close behind an individual's earlier death. With little knowledge available to protect their bodies from contamination, it would appear normal to dispose of the dead quickly and plead with spirits to leave the living and not jeopardize the perpetuity of the group.

Mourning rituals, while left largely to the female population are extremely common. Women among the Plains Hunters, hack or slash their arms, legs and face. Some may even cut off an ear. Both men and women may be expected to mutilate their bodies if they suffered the loss of a close kin, most certainly should a man have lost a son.[31] The Blackfeet women wear their oldest clothes, cut their hair and smear their faces with white clay. They may scratch the calves of their legs with sharp pieces of flint causing blood to flow and dry in rivulets.

---

[27]   E. Adamson Hoebel, op.cit. p.86.

[28]   Robert Tonkinson, op.cit. p83.

[29]   Robert Knox Denton, op.cit. p.90.

[30]   Frances F. Berdan, "The Aztecs of Central Mexico: An Imperial Society", N.Y. Holt, Rinehart and Winston, Inc., 1982.

[31]   William W. Newcomb, Jr., op.cit., p.96

Some widows, too, chop off joints of their fingers.[32] The Cheyenne women cut off their hair, and cut gashes in their forehead. These women, if they wish to make an extravagant display of their grief move off alone to live in the bush in isolation for as long as a year.[33] Both sexes of the Maradudjara inflict bloody scalp wounds with sharp objects at hand. The widow and other related females cut their hair and anoint themselves with red ochre. They refrain from eating certain foods for a period of two years as well.[34] The Salish widow could not marry for a period of two to three years and was not allowed to sing or work during that period. The mourners in this society wore their oldest clothes to indicate the extent of their grief. The wife of a Copper Eskimo does not wash for a year, nor look at the sky or the sea, speaks just above a whisper and does not eat certain foods during that period. The Semang refrain from wearing face paint, singing, dancing and playing musical instruments.[35] The Tiwi mourners as distinguished from non-mourners must be fed due to the taboo preventing them from touching any food.[36] Many societies encourage friends and neighbors of the deceased to relieve the immediate kin of necessary chores. The Mardudjara and the Eskimo as well as other societies, do not call the name of the dead nor do they speak of the dead for a designated time.

Mourning customs are interpreted in various ways. Eskimos believe that self-denial or sacrifice will please the ghost, i.e. the spirit of the dead person. The adherence to the mourning customs

---

[32]   George Bird Grinnell, op.cit. p. 194.
[33]   E. Adamson Hoebel, op.cit. p.88.
[34]   Robert Tonkinson, op.cit. p. 85.
[35]   Dale V. Hardt, op.cit. p.95.
[36]   C.W.M.Hart and Arnold Pilling op.cit. p.91

minimizes and forestalls the evil powers of the ghost.[37] While there may be grounds for questioning whether primitive man suffers from guilt, - the self-denial and mutilation could be ways of lowering the level of guilt if it in fact did or does exist. Hoebel, in an effort to explain the drastic measures of the Cheyenne states that the mourning customs provide widows with the only masochistic outlet available. The effect of such behavior would cause warriors to take pity on the widow and organize a revenge expedition when the dead died as a result of battle wounds.[38]

Hunting and Gathering Societies appear to have more highly institutionalized patterns of the disposal of belongings than those related to the disposition of the body. Hoebel reports that when an average person is on the verge of death, members of the Cheyenne tribe listen for the wailing sounds denoting the death and, in some cases, before death takes place, run to grab what they can of the deceased's property. This is not the usual pattern, however. The Eskimo place personal belongings such as implements and weapons in the grave, should the deceased be interred. Contributions of furs and utensils become part of the family's possessions.[39] The Comanche place the corpse across the back of a horse, lead the horse to a natural cave and shoot it to be left with the corpse, the saddle, and other personal belongings of the deceased. The remaining possessions are burned.[40] Weapons of the male and utensils belonging to the female are buried with each, respectively in the Cheyenne tribe. Everything else is given to non-relatives.[41] The possessions of the Salish are given

---

[37]   Dale Hardt op.cit. 96
[38] E. Adanson Hoebel op.cit p. 88.
[39] Dale V. Hardt, op.cit. p. 96.
[40] George Bird Grinnell, op.cit.p.194.

to those in need of them. The home where the deceased lived is burned.[42] The Semang are required to bring all the deceased's possessions to the grave site and frequently mutilate it so that it can no longer serve any purpose.[43] The Washo either discard or burn all possessions of the deceased.[44] Pottery bowls found in burial sites in certain areas of the south and southwest have always been "killed", i.e. a hole had been knocked out of the bottom.[45] It is interesting that while there is a wide range of alternatives in the disposition of the body, there appears to be a rather rigid pattern for the disposal of the deceased's possessions within each tribe in this early phase of social organization. Material possessions, in Hunting and gathering Societies, inhibit ease in moving from campsite to campsite. Allowing an heir to inherit possessions and thereby accumulate goods would be counterproductive to both the individual and the social group in these nomadic societies. The response to the dilemma concerning the disposal of the "estate" appears to support the best interests of societal perpetuation.

Death Patterns Among Horticultural Societies

As there appears to be a likely correlation between the subsistence level and the societal responses to death in Hunting and Gathering Societies, a similar pattern of correlation can be detected in selected Horticultural Societies or Simple Agricultural Societies. These societies have mastered the seed revolution and do maintain gardens. Usually

[41] E. Adamson Hoebel, op.cit.p87.
[42] Dale Hardt, op.cit.p95.
[43] Robert Knox Denton, op.cit.p. 90-91.
[44] James F. Downs, op.cit.p.59.
[45] Paul S. Martin, George L. Quemby, Donald Collier, "Indians Before Columbus, Chicago: University of Chicago Press, 1947, p. 214, 394.

they remain in an area adjacent to the garden for a period of six to seven years. At the end of this period the garden is left to fallow and the group moves to a new vicinity where a new garden has been established. Some Horticulturists replenish the soil and have not moved for as long as anyone remembers. In either case, settlement is much more permanent than among Hunters and Gatherers, the food supply is more assured, the accumulation of goods is more evident, the stratification of the group by age, sex and power more prevalent, the social organization more rigidly structured. Sheer logic would support the speculation that an area might be designated as a place for the disposition of the body; that sharing of surplus food might result in ceremonial feasts; that material goods might have greater value and serve a more profound function in the funeral process; that when differentiation of disposition exists it might be based on age, sex, or power rather than the availability of alternatives; and that the total response be more tightly organized and highly ritualized. One might also anticipate that the readily available food supply would enhance the serenity and peaceful nature of the group. This, indeed, is not the case. The horticulturists are generally seen as the most vicious and ferocious of all groups classified on the basis of subsistence.

While infanticide is acceptable in Horticultural Societies, suicide of the elderly is not reported. Horticulturists are warriors. It may be that life expectancy is short and when an older man does survive, he may be valued for his knowledge and judgment. Too there are those unpleasant chores for which there are never enough individuals to fill. The Yanamamo, by way of example, give the chore of removing the flesh of the corpse from the bones to an elderly man. This is accomplished after the death of one who died as a result of an epidemic, after the flesh is well rotted.

Conclusions

Dying, as well as death, is a social event in these earliest of societies. The needs of the dying are met in patterned ways. In those societies where infanticide and suicide are accepted in a "matter of fact" way, little attention is given to disposal of the body or to a response reflecting conflict. Social responses become more complex and elaborate as the individual increases in value. Among many Hunting and Gathering Societies, there is no ritual provided in memory of the dead. However, there may be some structured behaviors to deny the ghost of tampering with those remaining. In Horticultural Societies an effort is made to include the dying during the dying process and social responses to the death are automatic. In these societies, where the individual has increased in value, greater emphasis is given to the male than the female and is further enhanced by the social status of the individual lost. The conflict resulting from the loss of a group member, is modified by physical mutilations or further deprivations of foods, physical discomforts or dress. Agricultural Societies continue these practices to a more or less extent and frequently have elaborate feasts to commemorate the dead. All these practices and more reflect the fact that death is not only biological but also social. The social system of the group has been disrupted and the patterned social responses are designed to enable a new structure to take place.

Chapter 4

Attitudes of Death in America

For many years, other than in religious connotations, death was not considered an appropriate topic for social conversation. Then in the 60's and 70's there was a plethora of published articles indicating a concern for the mental health of American society. Death was no longer viewed by society as a natural process but actually "denying" that death occurred.

In the 30's and 40's (more or less) death was acknowledged openly in a variety of ways. First and foremost, death took place in the home of the dying. The family surrounded the bedside and when possible, there was continued conversation with the dying. Grandchildren were invited to see Grandpa (or Grandma). There might have been last minutes concerns about the distribution of possessions and, in the case of a dying husband, concerns for the care of his surviving spouse. When the physician declared that death had indeed occurred, the

---

Undertaker was contacted. He came to the house with a Crepe to attach to the side of the door. The public was made aware of the fact that the family was in mourning. Their grief was to be acknowledged by the neighbors and passersby. They were encouraged to show respect for the dead.

The Undertaker also brought the embalming lounge to be set up in room which could be closed off to household traffic. He made frequent trips to check on the embalming process. Meanwhile Death Notices were mailed to individuals who could not be contacted locally. This then necessitated that the funeral be delayed until such time as the notices could be delivered by the Postman.

Meanwhile there were various details that had to be addressed by the mourners. Men, closely related to the deceased wore a black tie and black arm bands while, women closely related wore a black dress, a black veil, a black hat and black gloves for the funeral. Women's dress shops carried a variety of styles from which to choose. Men continue to wear the black tie and armband for a short period of time. The women, however continued to wear the black dresses for as long as a year in some cases.

The Historical Perspective

Phillip Aries in "The Hour of Our Death" (19--) identified four phases of societal attitudes to death indicating a change in attitude taking place throughout history. The "Tamed Death" was the earliest of these and in some respects the event of dying and death during this period had similarities to the agricultural patterns reported in the ethnographic studies. During this period the individual was forewarned of his/her impending death and took necessary steps to accept it and embrace it. Legends of the past tell us of Roland, Tristan, and especially Lancelot who removed his weapons, lay down quietly on the ground with arms spread out to form a cross and his head facing east toward Jerusalem and died. (Sometime during the 12th and 13th century Christians changed this posture. The dying Christian crossed their arms on their chest and faced Heaven, the Jews faced The Jerusalem Wall.) The important phenomenal of this stage was the control one had over his own death. Being forewarned enabled him to carry out his final steps in his demise. More specifically, the dying had the opportunity to plan a public ceremony. He could bring together numerous comrades and family members to share his feelings about his life experiences and association with them and to express concerns he had in relation to them. It also gave the members within the circle time to share their feelings with the dying member. The dying could reflect on his regrets to leave them, had time to pray and ask for forgiveness and think about God. After these needs were met, the dying silently awaited their death. According to Aries, during the 18th century, physicians complained about the overcrowding of the bedroom with families, children and neighbors. However, there was little emotional response during the event. The living and the dying co-existed and accepted death as a natural part of life.

During the 11th and 12th centuries according to Aries, the common acceptance of death and the bedside rituals changed. This phase of historic change Aries entitled "One's Own Death." The "accounting book" came into existence in which the good behavior as well as the evil behavior was recorded. The good and the bad were to be separated. God was very much a part of the dying scene, there to observe the fight between the good and evil forces in their struggle to take possession of the dying man's soul and to view the conduct of the dying in the midst of that struggle. The record ended on the individual's last day in this world including his attitude during the final moments. He faced judgment accordingly.

The family continued to be part of the scene and supernatural beings were present.

Children were not shielded from the dying process and were socialized with the understanding that judgment was unavoidable. The decomposition of the body was viewed as a sign of failure, a sign of a life lived in rejection of the good. The collective body believed that the physical body of all "good" men was to be awakened on the day of the second coming of Christ and the risen physical body would live in Paradise forever.

The rituals at this stage of history became much more emotional than in prior years. The lifetime of the dying was reminisced. Nevertheless, the dying continued to be in control of his death.

During the 16th to the 18th century group members became more concerned with another's death as opposed to their own as was true in the 11th-15thth centuries. Aries termed this phase "Thy Death." Whereas death had been seen as a natural event with the acknowledgement that all must die, in the 18th century death was seen as an aberration. The family structure during this period was based on strong feelings and attachments for its members. Death meant the tearing apart of the closely-knit group. Family and friends continued to enter the chamber of the dying, but the relationship was tense and very emotional. During "One's Own On Death", the dying expressed his religious faith, his sadness in parting with his possessions, his feelings for those especially important to him and his relationship to God. His wishes and concern for the future was dealt with the family and associates gathered together by his bedside. A drastic change took place during the 18th century. While feelings for members were more apparent, the dying member distrusted the heirs and a professional were called in to read the will and execute it. During the second half of the century, wills became secularized.

The dying member could speak confidentially to those close to him, but the responses of the members about him changed considerably. "Thy Death" was feared. Mourning was exaggerated. The survivors were unwilling to part from the dead. Family cemeteries became popular. These characteristics were particularly apparent in England and America.

Suggestions to continue a semester seminar:

The Cemetery: Colonial, Victorian, Romantic, Capitalism, Realism

Special Cases

A Child's Perception of Death

Suicide

Euthenasia

Life After Death

Bibliography

Thomas Rhys Williams, Introduction to Socialization, St. Louis: C. V. Mosby, 1972, p. 11. 2.

Jerome Bruner, Toward a Theory of Instruction, New York: Norton 1968, p. 74. 3.

Nicholas S. Timasheff and George Theodorson, Sociological Theory, N. Y.: Random House, 1976, p. 69. 4.

Gretel H. Pelto and Pertti J. Pelto. The Cultural Dimension of the Human Adventure, N. Y.: MacMillan, 1979, p. 42. 5.

Williams, op.cit. p. 125. 6.

C. W. Hart and Arnold R. Pilling, The Tiwi of North Australia, N. Y.: Holt, Rinehart and Winston, Inc., 1960 p. 18. 7.

Interviews with Professor R. P. Sharma, Regional Officer, U. S. Educational Foundation in India; Professor D. P. Apte, Registrar, Gokhale Institute of Politics and Economics, Pune; and Mr. S. A. Patanker, Tilak College of Education, Pune, July 1980. 8.

Gerhard Lenski and Jean Lenski, Human Societies, N. Y.: McGraw-Hill, 1978, p. 103. 9.

Edward Weyer, Jr., The Eskimos: Their Environment and Folkways, New Haven: Yale University, 1932, p. 249. 10.

Ronald Rohner and Evelyn Rohner, The Kwakiutl: Indians of British Columbia, N. Y.: Holt, Rinehart and Winston, 1970, p. 52. 11.

Dale V. Hardt, Death: The Final Frontier, N. J.: Prentice-Hall, 1979, p. 95. 12.

John Nance,The Gentle Tasaday, N. Y.: Harcourt Brace Jovanovich, 1975, p. 396. 13.

C.W. Hart and Arnold R. Pilling, op. cit. p. 90. 14.

Hardt, op. cit. p. 95. 15.

William S. Laughlin, Aleuts: Survivors of the Bering Land Bridge, N. Y.: Holt, Rinehart, and Winston, 1980, p. 89. 16.

E. Adamson Hoebel, The Cheyennes: Indians of the Great Plains, N. Y.: Holt, Rinehart, and Winston, 1960, p. 86. 17.

Clark Wissler, Indians of the United States, N. Y.: Doubleday and Co., Inc., 1940, p. 304. 18.

George Bird Grinnell, Blackfoot Lodge Tales, Lincoln, Neb.: University of Nebraska Press, 1962, p. 194. 19.

E. Adamson Hoebel, The Political Organization and Law- Ways of the Comanche Indians, Menasha, Wis.: American Anthropological Association, 1940, p. 112. 20.

William W. Newcomb, Jr., North American Indians: An Anthropological Perspective, Cal.: Goodyear Publishing Co, Inc., 1974, p. 118. 21.

Robert Knox Denton, The Sema: A Nonviolent People of Malaya, N. Y. :Holt Rinehart and Winston, Inc. 1979, p. 90 22.

Robert Tonkinson, The Mardudjara Aborigines: Living the Dream in the Australia's Desert, N. Y.: Holt, Rinehart and Winston, 1978, p. 83. 23.

Dale V. Hardt, op. cit. p. 95. 24.

Lewis Henry Morgan, The Indian Journals, 1859-62, Ann Arbor: The University of Michigan Press, 1959, p. 82-83. 25.

James R. Downs, The Two Worlds of the Washo, N. Y.: Holt, Rinehart and Winston, Inc., 1966, p. 59. 26.

Lewis Henry Morgan, op. cit. p. 83. 27.

E. Admason Hoebel, op. cit. p. 86. 28.

Robert Tonkinson, op. cit. p. 83. 29.

Robert Knox Denton, op. cit. p. 90. 30.

Frances F. Berdan, The Aztecs of Central Mexico: An Imperial Society, N. Y.: Holt, Rinehart and Winston, Inc., 1982, p. 94. 31.

William W. Newcomb, Jr., op. cit. p. 96. 32.

George Bird Grummell, op. cit. p. 194. 33.

E. Adamson Hoebel, op. cit. p. 88. 34.

Robert Tonkinson, op. cit. p. 85. 35.

Dale V. Hardt, op. cit. p. 95. 36.

Dale V. Hardt, op. cit. p. 96. 37.

Robert Knox Denton, op. cit. p. 93. 38.

C. W. M. Hart and Arnold R. Pilling, op. cit. p. 91. 39.

Dale V. Hardt, op. cit. p. 96. 40.

E. Adamson Hoebel,op. cit. p. 88. 41.

E. Adamson Hoebel, ibid. p. 86. 42.

Dale V. Hardt, op. cit. p. 96. 43.

George Bird Grimmell, op. cit. 194. 44.

E. Adamson Hoebel, op. cit. 87. 45.

Dale V. Hardt, op. cit. p. 95. 46.

Robert Knox Denton, op. cit. p. 90-91. 47.

James F. Downs, op. cit. p. 59. 48.

Paul S. Martin, George L. Quemby, Donald Collier, Indians Before Columbus, Chicago: University of Chicago Press, 1947, p. 214, 394. 49.

Napolean A. Chagnon, Yanomamo: The Fierce People, N.Y.: Holt, Rinehart and Winston, Inc., 1977, 50.

Leopold Poposil, The Kapauku Papuans of West New Guineau, N. Y.: Holt, Rinehart and Winston, Inc. 1978, p. 70. 51.

Karl Heider, Grand Valley Dan: Peaceful Warriors, N. Y.: Holt, Rinehart and Winston, Inc. 1979, 122. 52.

Edward P. Dozier, The Kalinga of Northern Luzon, Phillipines, N. Y.: Holt, Rinehart and Winston, Inc., 1967, p. 52. 53.

Edward P. Dozier, ibid p. 52. 54.

Karl Heider, op. cit. p. 126. 55.

Louis C. Faron, The Mapache Indians of Chile, N Y.: Holt, Rinehart and Winston, Inc. 1968, p. 95. 56.

Bruce G. Trigger, The Huron Farmer: Farmers of the North, N. Y.: Holt, Rinehart and Winston, 1969, p. 105. 57.

Bruce G. Trigger, ibid. p. 107. 58.

Thomas Rhys Williams. The Dusun: A North Bormeo Society, N. Y.: Holt, Rinehart and Winston, 1965, p. 18. 59.

Edward P. Dozier, op. cit. p. 52. 60.

William A. Lessa, Ulith: A Micronesian Design for Living, N. Y.: Holt, Rinehart and Winston, Inc., 1966, p. 112. 61.

Karl Heider, op. cit. p. 127. 62.

Louis C. Faran, op. cit. p. 94. 63.

Michael J. Harner, The Jivaro, N.Y.: doubleday, 1972, p. 166 64.

Shirley Lindenbaum. Kuru sorcery, Cal: Mayfield Publishing co., 1979, p. 22. 65.

Napoleon A. Chagnon, op. cit. p. 50. 66.

Louis c. Faron, op cit. p. 97. 67.

Bruce G. Trigger, op. cit. p. 106. 68.

Karl Heider, op. cit. p. 123. 69.

William U. Newcomb, Jr., North American Indians: An Anthropological Perspective, Cal: Goodyear Publishing, Co. Inc., 1974, p. 47. 70.

Leopold Poposil, op. cit. p. 70. 71.

Karl Heider, op. cit. p. 124. 72.

Bruce G. Trigger, op cit. p. 106. 73.

Edward P. Dozier, op cit. p. 53. 74.

William A. Lessa, op. cit. p. 113. 75.

Leopold Paspicil, op. cit. p. 69. 76.

Louis c. Faron, op. cit. pl. 94. 77.

John Middleton, The Lugbara of Uganda, N. Y. : Holt, Rinehart and Winston, 1965, p. 68. 78.

T. O. Beidelman, The Kaguru: A Matrilineal People of East Africa, N. Y.: Holt, Rinehart and Winston, Inc., 1971, p. 114. 79.

Hilda Kuper, The Swazi: A South African Kingdom, N. Y. : Holt, Rinehart and Winston, 1963, p. 58. 80.

Beverly L. Chinas, The Isthmus Zapotocs: Women's Roles in Cultural Context, N. Y.: Holt Rinehart and Winston, Inc., 1973, p. 60. 81.

Michael Kearney, The Winds of Ixtepeji: World View and Society in a Zapotec Town, N. Y.: Holt, Rinehart and Winston, Inc., 1972, p. 54. 82.

Norma Diamond, K'un Shen: A Taiwan Village, N. Y.: Holt, Rinehart and Winston, Inc., 1969, p. 49. 83.

T. O. Beidelman, op. cit. p. 115. 84.

John Beattie, Bunyoro: An African Kingdom, N. Y.: Holt, Rinehart, and Winston, Inc., 1960, p. 65. 85.

Norma Diamond, op. cit. p.86.

John Middleton, op. cit. p. 66. 87.

Beverly L. Chinas, op. cit. p. 60. 88.

Paul R. Turner, The Highland Chontal, N. Y.: Holt, Rinehart and Winston, Inc., 1972, p. 39. 89.

Beattie, op. cit. p. 65. 90.

John Middleton, Op. cit. p. 67. 91.

T. O. Beidelman, op. cit. p. 114. 92.

T. O. Beidelman, ibid. p. 115. 93.

John Middleton, op. cit. p. 71. 94.

Paul R. Turner, op. cit. p. 39. 95.

Beverly L. Chinas, op. cit. p. 62. 96.

John Beattie, op. cit. p. 65. 97.

Norma Diamond, op. cit. p. 45. 98.

John Beattie, op. cit. p. 65. 99.

T. O. Beidelman, op. cit. p. 116. 100.

Paul R. Turner, op. cit. p. 40. 101.

Beverly L. Chinas, op. cit. p. 63. 102.

Hilda Kuper, op. cit. p. 58. 103.

Norma Diamind, op. cit. p. 48. 104.

T. O. Beidelman, op. cit. p. 114. 105.

Norma Diamond, op. cit. p. 50. 106.

John Beattie, op. cit. p. 65. 107.

Hilda Kuper, op. cit. p. 58. 108.

Beverly L. Chinas, op. cit. p. 66. 109.

John Middleton, op. cit. p. 67. 110.

William Bascom, The Yoruba of Southwestern Nigeria, N. Y.: Holt, Rinehart and Winston, Inc., 1969, p. 65-69. 111.

T. O. Beidelman, op. cit. p. 116. 112.

E. Adamson Hoebel, op. cit. p. 88. 113

Acknowledgement: Jerry T. Hancock